The Signature Series

__065__ of 100

Praise for *Tortillera*

"The poems in Caridad Moro-Gronlier's moving and multi-valent debut *Tortillera* travel great distances, within the self and beyond. By turns lyric and narrative, tender chronicle meets tough reckoning, the speaker of this unflinching mem-oir-in-verse plumbs 'the canyon of want' as daughter, wife, mother, and ultimately, as the authentic queer woman she was meant to become—'buried for eons, glorious, final-ly found.'"

—Julie Marie Wade, author of *When I Was Straight* and
Just an Ordinary Woman Breathing

"'I wasn't *la niña bonita* / my parents wanted,' says the speaker early on. 'I was the mouthy one'—and what a ride-of-a-book this is, our narrator 'croon[ing] words on com-mand' to flesh out a sometimes heart-wrenching journey . . . from '[lying] within a canyon of want' to being 'talked into a pool hall / strung out on tequila and cafecito.' Let's call it deliciously transgressive—where someone 'poured red velvet into my glass' for the sake of this 'infection we call love' that may lead one to utter: 'the ache that is your name' and experience the 'warble // of loss.' In short, *Tortillera* 'is a thing of beauty / but not in the way / of Barbie dolls'!"

—Francisco Aragón, author of *After Rubén*

Tortillera

TORTILLERA

poems

Caridad Moro-Gronlier

Texas Review Press | Huntsville, Texas

LIMITED EDITION

Printed and Bound in the United States of America
First Edition Copyright: 2021

Library of Congress Cataloging-in-Publication Data

Names: Moro-Gronlier, Caridad, 1969- author.
Title: Tortillera : poems / Caridad Moro-Gronlier.
Other titles: TRP Southern poetry breakthrough series.
Description: Limited edition. | Huntsville, Texas : TRP: The University
    Press of SHSU, [2023] | Series: The TRP Southern poetry breakthrough
    series ; Florida | First published by Texas Review Press in 2021.
Identifiers: LCCN 2022040903 | ISBN 9781680033427 (cloth)
Subjects: LCSH: Cuban American lesbians--Poetry. | Florida--Poetry. |
    LCGFT: Lesbian poetry. | Poetry.
Classification: LCC PS3613.O755219 T67 2023 | DDC 811/.6--dc23/eng/20220914
LC record available at https://lccn.loc.gov/2022040903

Published by TRP: The University Press of SHSU
Huntsville, Texas 77341
texasreviewpress.org

For my wife, Elizabeth, my first and best reader.

May I write words more naked than flesh,
stronger than bone, more resilient than
sinew, sensitive than nerve.

—Sappho

CONTENTS

III.

Entry

Tortillera, n.
Pronunciation: Spanish /tor-ti-lle-ra/, Spain, Latin, Central and South America, U.S.
Forms: Torti, Torta, Tort, Tortilla
Etymology: <Latin *tortus* (*twisted*), <Spanish *torta*, <German *que*, <English *queer*. Compare French *tortille*.
Origin: From term *torticera* (*tortious*), derived from Latin *tortus*, with the meaning of crooked, twisted, etc.; *torticera*, a highbrow word, by a process of popular etymology pronounced wrongly as *tortillera* by their phonetic similarity as in "*she is tortillera*" instead of "*she is torticera*" by an error in pronunciation.

Synonyms: *amaricada, arepera, bollera, bollo, buchona, cachapera, cambuja, camionera, come coños, desviada, ententida, fricatriz, hombruna, invertida, juega tenis, kiki, lechuga, lela, lencha, lesbiana, machorra, marimacha(o), obvia, sáfica, sopaipilla, tijeras, tribada, trola, troquera, virago, webiá, zapatona*

1.

a. Homosexual woman; lesbian.
I outed myself as a tortillera at Noche Buena dinner last Christmas and I was roasted along with the lechón.

b. Transatlantic traveler term known to connect homosexuality with the beginning of homophobia; refutes all sexual and onomatopoeic explanations (i.e., the supposed equivalency between the clapping sound made from kneading corn pancakes to the sound made during lesbian sex) as seen through the consideration of homosexual behavior as something twisted, deviant, first referenced in 1830 in the Spanish-French dictionary by M. Nuñez de Taboada, published in Madrid, in which the French word *tribade* is translated as *tortillera* and defined as "a woman who abuses another."

My mother did not allow me to play softball in high school because the coach was a tortillera and she didn't want me to end up a tortillera too.

c. Derogatory slang that denotes deviant, twisted behavior, the lowest form of female debasement, term known to induce emotional distress such as shame and self-loathing, as well as physical symptoms including, but not limited to, anorexia, bulimia, cutting, dermatitis, depression, enuresis, flushing, gastritis, heart palpitations, hyperhidrosis, insomnia, irritable bowel syndrome, kyphosis, lethargy, malaise, mania, nausea, nightmares, OCD, panic attack, paranoia, rash, rosacea, scarring, sleepwalking, stuttering, tachycardia, tongue biting, teeth gnashing, thinning hair, ulcers, vomiting, xerostomia.

Better my daughter be dead than a disgusting tortillera.

2. Female producer and seller of maize pancakes.

According to Adolfo Sanchez Vazquez, upon the arrival of Spaniards exiled to Mexico due to the Civil War, some were greeted by a sign that read "El sindicato de Tortilleras les da la bienvenida!," which caused someone to quip, "This is a very cosmopolitan country if even tortilleras have a union!"

I.

]You will remember
] For we in our youth
did these things

—Sappho

Unpacking the Suitcase

After West Side Story Upside Down, Backwards, Sideways and
Out of Focus (La Maleta de Futriaco Martinez) by ADÁL, 2002

I. Snippets of West Side Story, Los Angeles, CA, 1974

This is how you learn you are not an all-American girl.

Once a year you watch *West Side Story*
on the screen of your parents' 1974 Zenith
and catch a glimpse of yourself on television.
You are the firstborn gringa in the family.
Your English is perfect, but you're not
like your friends. You don't go to slumber parties
or play-dates, you don't join the Brownies
or take ballet, but once a year you get to
live in Technicolor and root for the Sharks
because they speak Spanish too.

You're taught there is safety in numbers,
you move in packs, sibling cloistered, in
an apartment building just like Maria's,
cousins and tías on every floor, duennas
in batas de casa adept at concealing battalions
of Playtex Cross Your Heart bras, black lace
slips that slide off the shoulder, the delicate
mauve of a fading bruise.

During the mambo scene, your mother dances
around your living room, tells you to watch her,
shows how to control the Hula-Hoop of your skirt

so that the crinolines she has pinned to your PJs
orbit around your hips, ruffled panties a flash
and blur. Makes you promise not to tell your father
what you've learned.

Like Anita, your mother knows her way around
a bolt of cloth, but you say nothing of how
she sews the clothes you wear, how after work
she comes home to your dresses, red-cushioned
pushpin corsage at her wrist, alchemy
of thread and Simplicity Patterns
spun into gold standard replicas
fit for the girl you want to be
but aren't.

II. Sound Bites: "En Mi Viejo San Juan" as Sung by Brenda Feliciano

My father makes me learn to play
"En Mi Viejo San Juan" on the guitar.
Makes me earn the lessons he pays for,

makes me croon the words on command
so I can perfect the version he prefers—
Brenda Feliciano, her warble

of loss—
the third language
we speak at home.

(Adios, adios, adios)

It doesn't matter that
my father is from Havana
or that he's never seen San Juan.

What matters is how he weeps
when I begin to sing, a keen
that careens into a wail I replicate

but cannot understand. I am
thirteen and have never lost anything,
except his approval.

I am thirteen and want
nothing more than to escape
the ache in his house, escape

to where I will long
for nothing,
especially his love.

(Adios, adios, adios)

III. What I Told Pedro Pietri about My Father at the Nuyorican Cafe

He was never late
He didn't have a car
He worked

He walked to work
He was always on time
He was on time the day the wheel spinner took his finger
He was on time on the morning the foreman was late
He was on time on the morning the foreman forgot to check
    his machine
He heard his finger jam the machine before he saw it severed
He saw his finger spinning in the wheel before he felt the
    pain of its loss
He joked that the wheel spinner ate his finger before he ate
    his breakfast
He joked that he should have called in sick
He joked because he had no sick days
He apologized for breaking the machine
He apologized for his blood, how it tie-dyed the wheel
He apologized after he fainted
He apologized for the mess his mangled hand left on the
    floor
He apologized to Hector who was sent to clean up the mess
He was twenty-one
The wheel spinner was older than he was
The foreman said it was an accident
The foreman said The Company was not at fault
The Company offered him 1,500 dollars
He thought 1,500 dollars was a fortune
The foreman told him 1,500 dollars was more than the going
    rate for a single finger
He thought 1,500 dollars was more than he deserved
He did not say the foreman was usually late
He did not say the foreman was usually hungover

He did not say the foreman had to rig the machine every
    morning
He said it was an accident
He said the foreman was not at fault
He said The Company was not at fault
He signed the No-Fault Agreement
He signed it with his left hand
He signed the check
He signed it with his left hand
He walked home with fifteen 100-dollar bills in his pocket
He bought a solid gold ID bracelet branded with his name to
    remind him of who he was
He went back to work as soon as they let him
He was never late

Analfabeta

It took a while for Abuela to figure out that an F
on my report card did not stand for *Fantástico*,
her experience with school limited to fourth grade
back in the days of wooden rooms and rulers that beat
knowledge into those bold enough to opt for ignorance.

Abuela kept what she could from el colegio en el campo
arithmetic, the alphabet, penmanship that wobbled
long before her arthritis set in. She would not stand for less
than my best, which is why she beat my ass with her
    chancleta
when she learned I'd been lying about my ease with fractions
    and PE.

You would have thought her a dignitary the day she walked
into my 6th-grade classroom, staccato heels, her good black
    dress
ironed crisp as a dollar, all for a date with Mrs. Dempsey
who looked at us down the long slope of her nose and began
to tear me down in tea-time tones that forgot to mention

she sometimes slipped and called me Spic, how she pounced
when I spoke to my friends in Español. Abuela caught most
of the words Dempsey lobbed her way but didn't say a thing,
just glared at me every second she endured the shame of
my shortcomings, as personal as the fine stitch of her heir-
    loom DNA,

as if she alone were to blame for the thrust of my chin, the
    purse

of my lips, the crossbones of arms I strapped to my chest as
    the words
too smart for her own good lingered in the air like the bells
that ruled our days, which is when Abuela finally stood, said
    the words
that set me straight——*Neber too esmart, mi niña, neber too*
    esmart!

Arbolito in el Exilio, 1979

They all wore red, but you wore green and stared
at me all night because neither one of us belonged.

Tupperware ladies welcomed you, shared recipes
for aspic, papier-mâché, fed you watercress

fingers on fancy Chinet plates and you tried
to blend in, but you weren't frumpy or fifty

the kind of bouffant beauty who smiled big
but never offered a cheek, like you did, leaning in

at hello, shimmer of tinsel, foreign as outer space,
the new Cuban girl on the block, struggling to mask

your accent and sing along with Bing, the heartbroken
Americano who also wept for somewhere else.

You understood why I longed to discard my needles,
fill the house with evergreen, shrug off the indignity

of plastic, a lifetime of waiting tucked away in the attic
safe as your exile where you dreamed of Los Reyes Magos,

Noche Buenas back home, women serving plate after
    plate—
lechón, frijoles, yuca, arroz.

Topography

After Ana Mendieta, Siluetas Series, *1980*

You have come to make sense
of this land, to lie within
a canyon of want, stake a spot
of stone with the weight of your bones.

You have come to plant
your body in this cracked earth,
parched streambed that survives
on the memory of water.

You have come as if this place
could sustain you, retain the whole
of you, the stamp and edge of you,
but Los Estados Unidos will never be home.

You have come to leave
your impression in the ground,
a reminder of what is left after
the stripping away of root, seed, soil—

cavern, chronicle, chasm.

Inheritance

Fresh off the Freedom Flights from Havana, my father,
fifteen and hungry, ground copper against concrete,
shaved pennies into dimes, fooled the cigarette
machines at Jackson Sr. High into putting out packs
of Camels he'd unload at lunch, just enough
for a carton of Carnation milk or a juicy Red Delicious.

He never forgot poverty's rumble, its careen
through the cavern of his abdomen, hunger
a rubber mallet thudding against his ribcage
as he scraped away scraps of food defiled
by ash and butts on the graveyard shift
at Wolfie's on Collins, where his boss, Buddy,
never let him sample the blue-plate specials

he could not afford to buy, his tips dependent
on blond waiters who called him wetback
and slipped him less than ten percent. There

he learned to love the heft of coins, amassed
a legacy in jars—Krugerrands, doubloons, silver
dollars we dig up now, eager to cash in
on the sum of his fear, keep it close, just in case.

Wet Foot, Dry Foot, 2002

We watch the rush hour spectacle
from our living room exile,
plush and merciless as the helicopters
that swivel between palm trees and swoop in
for the next great shot.

Amid feet pounding pavement, bodies
scatter across the Rickenbacker Causeway
but only her polished onyx face anchors the screen—
dressed up for a new life in buttercup yellow organza
awash on the gangplank, her soles sway
sheathed in lace-rimmed socks, white patent leather
Mary-Janes too big for her feet, starched
ribbons braided through her hair.

We don't ask what it cost,
her Sunday best—

not Abuela who buys those same itchy dresses at La Canas-
    tilla Cubana
for my cousins in Havana now that lace and church have gone
    black market;

not Papi who once ran from hammer-fisted rednecks
eager to knock his accent right out of his mouth;

not Mami who collects pantyhose and Kotex
for her best friend, Teresita, whom she had to leave behind.

It's easier that way, easier to overlook her

space on the freighter, so much like the one
that ferried cousin Pepito to Key West during El Mariel,
easier to complain about the invasion of Key Biscayne
where work-wizened nannies speak Creole now
that Español has moved into the zip code.

We do not speak of travesties—
Wet Foot, Dry Foot,
white face, black face,
tic-tac-toe of policy.

We do not ask if she dreams of griot,
soil culled vegetables, a brand-new doll
dressed in buttercup yellow.

Only human when it comes to our own,
we watch and know she'll be returned
to Port-au-Prince, sea weary, sweat-drenched
dress a ruined souvenir strapped to her back.

What I Should Have Said, Instead

For Zelda

I took you to Arby's for lunch
to get you talking. Something about
that ten-gallon hat inspired courage
and you glowed like the cocuyos
we trapped in glass jars that summer
you were five and sure Papi was right
about everything, including me.

You unearthed confessions,
meteors that streaked past your lips.
Explosions—
I may not graduate.
We never use condoms.
He grabs, but almost never hits.

Geese do it too, tuck their heads
beneath a pall of fluff
to keep from noticing the danger
all around—Styrofoam cups
that fool babies into taking strangled bites,
silent alligators that prove lethal
beneath the green guise of indifference.

I ate your fries. Shoveled them down my throat
like a grave digger. I spun sugared sentences
into webs sticky with logic, but you swept them away
with bristles long practiced at the art of cleanup.

On the way home, I missed my chance
to get it right, missed the moment
when you asked me to go back
for the purse you'd forgotten on the table,
missed my chance to try again
as we pulled into the same parking spot
and walked through the same double doors
back to the moment when I got it all wrong,
missed the miracle of your purse, right
where you left it, still untouched, valuables intact.

I threw stones when I should have created
a pile, planted a rock garden, assembled
sentries to guard against erosion.
We could be there now—
weeds blooming into flowers,
talking about nothing,
nothing at all.

Compulsion: A Chronology

1969, Formula: 8:31 a.m. I emerge a mottled warrior, clotted milk cheesy, more than a little bruised. My mother is doped up on Demerol in room 564 while nurses hide their breasts beneath scrubs and do not think to take me to her when I cry. Bonding is not yet fashionable. They give me formula, a rubber nipple, quiet my wailing, ignore my need.

1972, Harina con huevo frito (fried eggs and cornmeal, Cuban style): It is lonely at Abuela's house for a girl who is three. I am warned to stay still, to stay seated, to clean my plate. She is mean, but I taste her love in the steam that rises from rose-studded porcelain bowls she collected one dish at a time from El Lucky Supermarket on Sepulveda Blvd. She strokes my hair as I pierce the glistening white veil with a single poke of my fork. Together we watch the yolk's molten yellow ooze. *Así comen las niñas buenas*, she says, approval thick as stew in my spoon.

1974, Concession Food: When I am five years old, my brother takes a stand inside my mother's womb and breeches his way into the world. My father does not don a paper gown; he takes me to the movies. We hunker down, watch *Mary Poppins* peddle her spoonfuls of sugar. I grip his hand as hard as I can bear. He indulges me like never before: popcorn and ice cream, a hot dog, *two* Cokes, a bag of sweet chocolate kisses I suck down to syrup before we get home. They help make the medicine go down.

1977, Ice Cream: Papi sits on the left, next to Carlito, then me, Mami on the right. I am eight, but feel much younger enveloped in a family sandwich on the couch as we watch *The Love Boat* and excavate ice cream from chipped mugs with crooked silver spoons. My parents rise for seconds, linger in the kitchen. Laughter follows them back to us. We all get seconds. There is joy in the smooth texture of churned milk laced with chocolate or pecans, whipped cream dollops, my parents' giggles. There is joy.

1982, Fried Chicken: Ari, the older girl down the street, invites me to join the throng about to head out to the beach. I beg and grovel at my mother's feet, run to the house in time to watch the van rumble to life in the driveway. On the ride over, there are no rules against talking or singing and when Ari cries out for 96X her father turns the knob on the radio without complaint. Cold fried chicken is passed around in grease-speckled tubs, no plates or napkins in sight. I eat with my hands. A sheen of fat dabs my chin. My third piece tastes like rebellion.

1984, Whopper with Cheese: Once we leave Midway Skating Rink, Burger King awaits. I eat because my father tells me not to. I eat because fast food leads to pimples and lard ass. I eat because Danny didn't ask me to slow skate even though Sandra told everyone he would. I eat because Patty got to make out with Johnny *and* his brother Tico and no one called her a slut. I eat because next to Patty, I feel like the ugliest girl alive. I eat because my father waits outside. I eat because I cannot cry with a Whopper in my mouth.

1987, Steak-umm Sandwiches with Oil-and-Vinegar Potato Chips: We plan the day carefully: transportation to and from his house, a note for me for the attendance office the next day, a box of condoms, sustenance for after. The sex is painful and bloody, then suddenly better and I feel conflicted. Already it feels too late for second chances. When we move to the kitchen to make lunch, the synchronicity of our movements soothes me—I slice the onions, he fries the paper-thin slices of Steak-umms so that the grease will not spatter onto my naked breasts. I hate the oil-and-vinegar chips he loves, but I say nothing and shove half the bag in my mouth. He strokes my face and says, *I knew you'd like it.*

1991, Wedding Cake with Buttercream Icing: I close my eyes as he brings the first taste of tradition toward my chin. I am not worried. He will not desecrate my makeup with buttercream icing. He is not that kind. His hands are gentle as he wipes away a crumb trapped on the surface of my lipstick, sticky as flypaper. He tells me I've never been more beautiful. He doesn't know that I've lived on celery and coffee for the past ten weeks, that by the time he peels off my dress, I will have gained two pounds from the booze and cake I ate with my hands in the kitchen when his back was turned. He mistakes the sweet rush of sugar glowing in my eyes for devotion.

1999, Phentermine: The pills are small and canary yellow, the closest thing to magic I've ever tried, so I pledge allegiance to the doctor who doles them out twenty-one at a time and come to depend on my golden beauties for pep and when the weight falls off my frame five pounds a weigh-in, my hair is the first to revolt, jumping ship in knotted fistfuls day after day in the shower until one night blood leaks out my nose and into my mouth and all I can think to do is lick away the evidence, tastiest thing I've had for weeks.

Puta

A certain slim-hipped Cuban boy
loved to wrap his tongue
around my brain,
poured obscenities
into my ear, words
I relished more than sex,
his Spanish Ricky Ricardo smooth—
Ay, Mami que rica estas—
the whole thing so wrong
it just made me wetter.

I wasn't la niña bonita
my parents wanted,
hands tangled
in suds and Brillo,
the kind of girl
who waited.

I counted the minutes
until lover boy called
and began
to stroke me down
the long length
of a coiled
telephone cord
stretched taut
into the laundry
room where I
became the girl
who let herself

be pushed into
the bathroom
at Woolworth's,
who said nothing
when laid flat
on a bench
in the Kiwanis dugout,
scant kisses
giving way
to Kleenex
that cleaned me
right up
for the quiet ride
home.

Quinceañera

Papi was too cheap
and Mami was too weak
to celebrate my quinces
in the grand fashion of some
of my friends who enjoyed parents
willing to mortgage the house
to peddle their pochungitas
into the right social circles,
but I didn't mind
because I had been to The Biltmore
where the super-rich threw soirees
and their money around, I'd seen
a particular Cuban-American princess
descend on a zirconium-studded
quarter moon that brought
forth a gasp from the guests
as the birthday girl smiled,
tipped back and cracked
her head on Carrera marble,
and once, at the Big Five Club,
where underwater ballerinas
could be had for an extra 300 bucks,
I saw a water nymph slam back three shots
of tequila right before show time, only
to pass out, the party busted up
by *el rescue*, hot paramedics who came
to resuscitate her back to the horror
of a shrieking fifteen-year-old, a thousand
layers of sodden lavender pooling at her feet,
the kind of chiffon I'd never seen

at Angelita's Salon de Quinces in Hialeah,
my favorite of all the quince spots,
where third-generation cousins gathered
for generic booze, dressed to the same
shabby nines, whooping it up as they waited
for the pink scallop shell to fall open
drawbridge slow and reveal a perky pearl,
rouged and posed on velvet, compulsory
crinolines and organza fanned out
beneath a crunchy taffeta gown,
trumpeting the arrival of yet another
available Cubanita, corseted assets
waiting to be plucked by any one
of the red-palmed boys lining the walls.

What the White Girl Asked at Our 20th High School Reunion

Why weren't we friends in school?

We weren't friends because I knew
you hung out in the American parking lot
unlike my boyfriend who parked his Stingray
in the Cuban one on the other side of school. Of course
I hung out there. Not that you would understand
why being his girl meant I could not
sit in your car at lunch and listen to
your Def Leppard, your Mötley Crüe,
leave him to fend for himself.

We weren't friends because he courted me
old school, couched beside my father
every Sunday while I served apprentice
to my mother, her eyes onion stung,
arms spattered with marrow and lard,
who worked at loving her place at the stove,
rules I had not learned how to break, yet.

We weren't friends because I envied
the way you weren't allowed to settle,
how you were encouraged to date
assorted breeds of boys who strutted
across the lawn to ring your bell. Your dad
waved his blessing out the door and didn't worry
because he taught you to discern, to choose

among them, taught you to drive
yourself, headlights set on more
than the slam of the same car door,
even if it was a Corvette.

II.

Mother dear, I
can't finish my
weaving
you may
blame Aphrodite.

—Sappho

At Least I Didn't Rape You

The wine we shared did it. He leaned
in and offered me some killer advice

because we both turned to look at the brunette
who passed our table on the way to the bathroom—

> *Since you're into chicks, you might as well*
> *think as if you had a dick.*

> *You have the power of preemptive strike,*
> *just follow her into the john.*

> *Wait until she leaves the stall then push her*
> *against the wall and take what you want.*

> *The truth is most guys won't admit it,*
> *but we'd knock you down*

> *if we had our way, spread your legs and plunge*
> *ourselves into any pussy we wanted.*

I consoled myself with all that could have been worse
than discovering he was the kind of man

my father would have loved for me to marry,
the kind of man who considered a woman nothing

more than split and cleft, orifice, cavity,
study in absence, a maw, a void,

worse than my girlhood, the litany of less
than my father hammered into me

his words exhumed, corroborated
by the pick and spade of his confession—

   Hija, a key that opens many locks is a master key,
         don't be the slut with the busted deadbolt.

   I'd rather kill you than let you
         turn yourself into a whore.

   At least I didn't rape you!
         Don't you know how lucky you are?

Somnambulism 101: Never Wake a Talker

For Sean

The first time my screams guillotined through your dreams
you leapt out of bed, pulse pounding conga around the room
you'd splurged on but couldn't afford.

We were in mint condition, then, our skeletons still
safe beneath the high luster of our sex-soaked skins
stretched taut over the model selves we sold one another—

too soon to unhinge my demons, too soon
to stir up trouble, too soon to confront the rumble
under the hood of our brand-new love.

My screaming didn't stop you—you let me speak from
    sleep,
fed me dawn one curtain slat at a time, the sun held captive
by soot-stained clouds dark as the fatigue that circled your
    eyes.

You rose in time to pull me out of myself, wiped
the terror from my unlined brow and vanquished
the nightmare I could not recount or recall.

You should have run then.

Cuban-American Lexicon

In Español
the word
for girlfriend
does not exist.

Instead
I was his
novia

(Hyphen)

intended
fiancé
bride

in training.
I was

neither
girl nor friend
to the boy
I chose

duty
down
the aisle
toward
the altar
where
novia

turned
into

spouse
consort
wife

(Hyphen)

esposa
in Español,
known also
to mean

shackle
manacle
handcuff.

Visionware

*When you're in love, every day is a reason to celebrate. Every meal
can be transformed into a special time to toast love, romance, and
your life together as a couple.*

—visions-cookware.com

There are things you should remember
    though you don't.

First night of our honeymoon
    my fists swirled around your head.

You pulled me from sleep
    blocked every blow I threw

as if the punches that landed
    didn't matter.

Eight days later we crossed the threshold
    you thinking of me

me thinking of ribbons, the silver
    wrapping I'd get to undo

in order to stock our kitchen with dreams
    I learned on the *Price is Right*

cut crystal, bone china, pots and pans
    of amber glass—

glass that never did learn how to burn,
    dinner scorched night after night.

What They Don't Tell You at the Baby Shower

You will be insane
far longer than you were pregnant—
lunatic with hormones, stretch-marked
skin a field of brambled scarlet.

You will leak,
stain every piece of clothing you wear, soft cloth now,
nipples cracked and bleeding, sustenance leached
away by the whine and pull of the breast pump.

You will know you never knew what it was to be exhausted,
bones etched with fatigue, fugue of feedings that fall
into short-reeled eye blink—Beaujolais and cigarettes, joy
until you jolt awake, remember you forgot the baby as you
        dreamed.

You will keep from shaking your child
who just won't stop crying. You will cower
in the closet, aglow in cell phone light,
crisis hotline on the other side.

You will grow afraid
of speeding cars and spinning spokes, of skid marks and sirens,
        of camp
counselors and men's rooms, of triple-dog-dares and high dives,
of high fives, laughter that lodges a jawbreaker in the throat.

You will long for an empty nest,
a white couch, a full glass of water, access to the remote
control, only to get it and wish you could return
to the mosaic of days you scrapbooked away.

Waiting to Be Discharged from the Maternity Ward

Consider the eyes of a boy who has the heart
to cram a Black Cat firecracker down the throat of a gecko.

Consider his hands, the giddy rush as he tries
and tries to light the match that will ice his blood.

Consider his laughter, the sound of explosion,
the slivers of lizard that land in his hair.

Consider my son, hours old, bruised
from the battle of breaking away from me

as I consider how to keep him
from stealing my lighter, from sneaking out back,

my love in his pocket,
M-80 in his hand.

Fourth Quarter

The Dolphins were winning for a change.
Parties paved a path toward a perfect season,
every Sunday measured by Marino's quick cannon
release, an assortment of aqua and orange
flung around a rotation of rooms united
in their hatred for the other side. Each week

I came and joined the wives, learned the couch-
to-kitchen shuffle but never wore a jersey
or the right colors, keys in hand at halftime,
the only beer run volunteer with no pennant
affixed to the rear car antenna.

I was there for you, but I never cheered or submitted
to the show of sentiment you held toward me
before every huddle, the hope you dispelled
after every hike. I didn't care about the score,
the offense, the defensive line

but you did. I tried but couldn't
get past what I believed—
game after game you did nothing
and called it a win, tallied your success
in sacks and yards you didn't run.
You didn't notice the clock
on us winding down.

Grilled

For Sean

When you asked me why I loved you early into the morning
of a fight that had raged all night, I couldn't answer, so I
   asked you
for a grilled-cheese sandwich, a request that left you slack-
jawed and baffled as if I'd asked for a divorce instead.

I was the mouthy one but could not explain
what I saw in those sandwiches—the delicate balance
of starch and protein, white bread that braved direct heat
for the sake of cheese so flimsy it was dependent

on a framework of flour to keep it from burning
on the unforgiving surface of a wounded frying pan.
I thought it settled when you gave me what I wanted,
toasted gold streaming light on all the damage we'd done.

I never did tell you how I felt,
just chewed it all up, the love
you served on our best china.
Never once offered you a bite.

That Night at the Rack 'Em Room

She talked me into a pool hall
strung out on tequila and cafecito
a gang of troubadours singing her praises
Damn, baby, you so fine!
as we walked in.

And she was. The kind of girl
who could get away
with Brazilian jeans.

I was coming off a bed-rest pregnancy—
skin stretched soft and loose
a half-racked game,
but with her, I felt bold
and pliable, shards of never-say-
never stuck in my throat.

I wasn't good at geometry,
how to control the crash
of the cue ball, the candy-coated orbs
that scattered into constellations
across the felt, but she kissed me
for luck and took her shot,
all angles and elbows,
taking them down
with a click of the stick,
the suckers who lined up
just to watch her
bend over that table,
hair blazing a trail

toward the sun that rose
out of the low-slung horizon
of her waistline, a single dot
that chased its tail into a swirl
I rode, knowing even then
everything spirals downward
but she kept shooting me smiles,
sinking one after the other,
me along with them.

At That Motel on 8th Street

her hands found me
engineers that surveyed
a landscape of thighs
pockmarked thoroughfares
stretched for miles
free of girders or steel
a thing of beauty
not in the way
of Barbie dolls
or silk orchids
but of railroad tracks
where rocks tremble
into pebbles
and grow wiser
like we did
in that borrowed room
where bliss broke
into minutes
we paid for
by the hour.

Labor Day, 2003, Lincoln Road, Miami Beach

There's a lot I remember
to forget, like the day we left
the kids with our husbands, both
too thunderstruck to protest our preference
for one another, simpler to sanction
our escape than block the door and stop us
from barreling down the road, purses
crammed with Xanax and Marlboros,
wallet-sized family portraits
tacky with toddler residue.

We both wore lipstick
and a safe distance
our bodies barely skimming
the surface of our desire.
We wandered in and out
of spaces where no one knew us
where no one cared that we gazed
at women on South Beach, where we
followed the smooching white-tanked girls
into Williams Sonoma and talked
them into registering
for the really good Dutch oven
before ducking into the Regal
half an hour early, so we could
hold hands in a theater drained of bright
where we swore we were ready
in the smoke and glare
of the movie screen.

I can say it now—

neither one of us
ever did give much away,
we packed and stored our castoffs,
like our husbands, bagged and waiting
to become of use again.

The Perfect Dress

I thought she looked good
in everything

    (imagine a fat girl like me
    shopping for a size 6)

but once she pressed me up
against the wall
of that plush, pink
dressing room
and kissed me
slow and deep,
I shook my head
after every dress
plied her with sequins
colors that did nothing
for her skin,
just to watch her
beckon with a cock
of the head that meant
I want you, sure
she'd fall into me
once the door clicked shut
behind us, which explains
why it took all day
to settle on
the very first one
she tried on.

It would take weeks
for her to mention
how she returned it,
how she stripped down
in the same dressing room
and modeled the outfits
her husband picked out
until he nodded his agreement
and decided on a black and blue
horror of a dress
she'd go on to wear
again and again.

Veteran's Day, 2005, Lincoln Road, Miami Beach

The day off made us think to try.

We wanted our slate clean.
Clean in an organic world
mulched world, composted,
recycled, hard and dirty world.

How do you return after waging a war?

Nothing to return to but what we knew before—
books you carried but never read,
my head turned away from you, face
against the glass, fighting the lure
of air on the other side of us, pretending
we could step back into who we'd never been,
couple in a frame contained by borders.

We could not outrun our dead
scattered across the cement,
no monument or statue
to commemorate our loss,
just hope, mangled to pieces.

We tried to rebuild
on a weakened foundation.
We sifted through rubble
and searched for remains,
as if fragments were enough
to hold us together.

For My Lover, Returning to Her Husband

After Anne Sexton

He is all there.
Disney promises,
fairy tales,
a cameo carved out of soap.

He has always been there.
Buff and bench-pressed,
primped, posed,
safe under glass.

I was an indulgence.
Cashmere draped across your thighs,
brownie binge after years of salad,
sweet cling peaches in February.

His piece fits your puzzle,
a perfect match. You see
to the girls, the dog,
the job, the mop,

he writes checks
that buy the best,
orders the chaos
you call your life,

marked by a Swiss watch
that minds minutes,
but not children
he seeded—

round and female,
your body filled with life
he put there,
cocky as God.

I give you back.
I give you permission—
for the lava inside him,
spewing on your thighs,

for the coward in him,
the drinker, the liar,
the teller of secrets
who wanted to watch,
for the pale scar on his nose,
for the prize that is his face,
for his strong man's arms
and seven white shirts,

for the vasectomy,
for the caretaker in you
who will consider compromise
when he burrows beneath you

and tugs on the brown
ribbons of your hair
to tie you up, tie you
to him, captive.

He is comfortable,
result of your childhood.
Climb him like Everest.
He is solid.

As for me, I am makeup.
I wash off.

What You Learn at the Track

Befriend the stable-hand. Yes, he is mud-mottled,
without silks, no cobalt or chartreuse to be found
in the barn, but he will teach you about gradations—
carob, umber, gingerbread, stone.

He will wave you onto the backstretch.
Reside in his silence at the rail, watch his favorite
three-year-old go all out on a blowout, a filly certain
to break maiden as soon as she's sprung from the gate.

After the cooldown, he will not lay odds, but hands.
He will run his fingers along the braille of her spine, decode
crinkle of snip and stripe, flare of star, ripple and swell
of tail, of flank, stroke the silken pennants of her ears.

Believe him when he tells you she's ready.
Place your bet minutes before the race, but be sure
you can afford what you put on her
because nothing is certain at the track—

no handicap, no program palm slap,
no prayer or chant, no shake up,
no curse, no whip, no scrub will coax
a front-runner that just won't run.

Nothing is certain but the promenade home.
Washout or winner, the stable is fragrant with oats
and molasses, feed sweet enough to overpower the stink
of the hot shoe, the hair singe that clings to the rafters.

Doing Without

In the rain
the room
darkens.

Learn to
be still
practice
the right
thing to do
the art
of composure

before he
gets home
and finds you

wrestling
the burden
down
to the ground

the burden
of doing
without

all
that cannot
save you.

Like Finger Sandwiches for Sumo Wrestlers

We used to
watch rush hour
seep into dusk

a single
cigarette
between us

but these days
you've quit smoking
and I've quit you

yet still
I ache
to take

what I can get,
a sliver
of not enough

because yes
my darling,
I am still starving

and wouldn't
you know
my coupons expired

a few months back,
which means I can't
afford to indulge

in satisfaction.
Better to forget
that cigarette

than have to wean
myself off you
one more time.

Raisins in the Stuffing

In the end
it would have come down to this—
where to go for Thanksgiving
and every November
we would have argued
over whose turn it was
to give in. Yes, we would
have drooled over our own
extravagant meal studded
with candied marigolds, French truffles
foraged by dogs trained to seek out
succulence only to give it back
again, and we'd tell each other
it was worth it, but in time
you would have thought
my mother's turkey
heavy on the garlic and
I would have complained
about the raisins
in your father's famous stuffing,
and on those Thursdays
when our ex-husbands
took their turn
feeding our children
we'd miss the noise
we'd taken for granted
and blame each other
for the silence
draped across the table
every other year.

Pruning Black-Eyed Susans on the Day of Our Divorce

Standing tall above the weeds my yellow girls flounce
green boas, turn their black eyes toward the clouds
and call for the sun that has slipped between linen sheets of
    sky.

They know that star cares little for down-turned faces
that swoon in the shade. They know there's no sense
pining away into a breakdown in the way of sunflowers—
pupils dilated, named for the lothario who's laid them low.

No, these Susies have their pride. They never stoop or
    submit,
never depend on straitjacket stakes to hold their heads up.

Coming Out to Mami

The cushions were beige,
dinner-partied, lived-on, scrubbed
clean as bleach would allow.

She spoke of remodeling,
zero percent interest at Rooms-To-Go,
how what couldn't be replaced
could be reupholstered.

We scoured fabric stores for bolts of cloth
dark enough to mask my stains,
strong enough to handle the strain
of starting over, as if perfect
squares of Enchantment Twill
could contain the messiness of living.

At home I slid scissors across material
she pressed into my hands. She watched
as I struggled for straight lines,
as I wept over jagged edges
I could not control.

She taught me to conceal irregularities,
to pin them down beneath
the sting of a staple gun,
smooth new skin over battered innards,
cushion after cushion reassembled,
both of us sure
I too could be remade.

III.

Once again love drives me on
that loosener of limbs
bittersweet creature against
which nothing can be done.

—Sappho

For Marlene, Who Asked Why I Switched
   Teams

One night at a party,
I haggled with my date
over a bottle of Pinot Noir
and a corkscrew he refused
to hand over. He wasn't
a prick, just a man
who thought the juice was his
because he brought me
and that's what guys do,
even though he didn't have a clue
how to handle the entry
or the swivel of the screw

    as if force
    could make anything
    come faster

he remained determined
despite the cork crumbling
into flecks, his failure
afloat the surface
of what he'd sullied.

A watchful brunette
crossed the room,
slid her body between us,
slid his hands off the wine,
slid her eyes down the bottle
and insinuated the tip of the screw

deeper by turns,
dislodged the cork
in one fluid motion
and poured red velvet
into my glass.

Later,
she spoke
of Portuguese cork trees,
trees so evolved
they had learned
to ward off disaster,
impervious to drought
or fire, the chew of termites
and chainsaws, trees capable
of renewing their skins.

I listened
beneath a canopy
of white sheets,
another
bottle
breathing
beside her bed.

Contemplation of a Name

Stay,
    see

        if I don't taste of guayaba and mamey, sweet guarapo
thick as my hips
        swaying sweaty Celia Cruz rhythms in black-seamed
stockings and Cuban
        heels.

Stay,
    see

        if I don't bring Dutch parrot tulips, orange and red
blazes for your table,
        Belgian chocolate pyramid stacked on Virginia's
dishes for your buffet,
        the essence of French lavender in a cobalt decanter
for your vanity.

Stay,
    see

        if I don't pick three trifectas in a row, read stray
pony hairs like tea leaves across
        the stable, kiss you at the window, winners.

Stay,
    see

        if I don't learn that song you love, pour it into your
ear, my voice sediment
        that sifts through your veins, silt that settles with
every beat.

Stay,
    see

        if I don't warrant the wait of avocados, figs, or kum-
quats, whatever

        your fruit—even the pomegranate, so delicious you
forgive its seeds.

I Did Not Take My Camera to Paris

A photograph passes for incontrovertible proof that a given thing
happened. The picture may distort; but there is always a presump-
tion that something exists, or did exist.

—Susan Sontag, *On Photography*

I was in love with you
and did not want
to commit us
to anything but memory,
sure I would never
need a souvenir
to document our elation.

I did not think to stop
the moment as it unraveled,
click past and distill it down
to digital, no shutter speed
sensitive enough to capture
the patina of fog
flanking the Eiffel Tower.

I did not want to tamper
with the truth
as I believed it—
we were perfect,
capable of conjuring calm
out of chaos, our lives
intersecting Metro lines,
colorful interchanges
we traced with our fingertips
on the map.

But oh, I should have
taken my camera to Paris,
should have created a testament
to the rain that did not deter us—
to your hands, nails crimson
to match my lips,
to our arrogance
on the plane as it taxied,
certain we could return.

Why Can't You Just Listen?

For Sean-Michael

I brought us to DC for Christmas to restring
your recollection, hang the fragile ornament
of our new family on a towering fir aflicker
with enough fluorescence to outlast us all,

but after three days of fossils & chicken
fingers & lost gloves, my hand tightened
into a vise around yours when your body
refused to yield to my quick-step schedule.

I was oblivious to the bounty I tried to hustle you past
as if a boy of seven, raised on palm trees
and balmy yuletides, could resist a snow-packed
pickup truck parked on Pennsylvania Ave.

Nothing I could do but snap
your picture—a moment
I chose to record
rather than inhabit.

We have to go
I said
and for the hundredth time that day—
Why can't you just listen?

As if I listened

to your laughter as it disappeared into the air,
to the crunch of ice as you ran, giddy with cold,
to your innocence as I calculated
how many minutes I could afford to allow.

When you think back on that day,
I hope you forget I scowled, remember
instead that for a moment I forgot myself,
smiled at you as snowballs flew.

The Really Good Dutch Oven

is Dijon yellow
lacquered enamel handed down
brighter than anything so old
has a right to be. Cast iron
behemoth, sentry amid uniform
Teflon gray. Fire-forged
depository that confesses
only once you lift the lid.
Veneer lined and cracked
but intact, remnants, what remains
after succulence—memory, years
of meals seared hot enough to stain,
no scrub pad, no elbow grease,
no will enough to remove
the residue of what once
sustained us.

Memento Mori

The ghost
of your cheek
still cleaves to
the blanched wall

      your portrait
      a flutter
      of hands

unencumbered by color

      face blurred
      to gray

   in rooms I emptied of you. Laughter

distilled to quiet

  a scatter

      of prints
      pressed to glass

  pane

I put away
long before
the dust
took hold.

I Don't Eat Plums Anymore

I could call you
but either way
there'd be too much

to break
to fix the ache
that is your name.

A good day is measured
in minutes I have
not thought of you.

All this to say
the tree we planted
has borne fruit

but I misplaced the recipe
for plum preserves
you left behind.

I have forgotten
you were so cold
not ever as sweet.

Uncoupled

The morning she flung the earrings she gave
me out the door and onto the grass

I dropped to my knees
and tried to recover

diamonds from a patch of earth
battened down by dirt and rain.

When I found one,
post and back intact,

I saw it as a sign—
we too could be saved,

we two could regain
what we both had discarded.

She watched me there,
stooped from the search

denim knees besotted with mud,
stains I never did get out

and we both know what remains—
one widowed earring

waiting to be repurposed
into pendant, stickpin, brooch,

but what I can't recall is why
I stopped the search

before I found what was lost,
why I decided I'd had enough

or why she didn't search too.

Taking the Sunrise Tunnel

Call this your life—
passageway gouged in the ground,

cylinder burrowed in earth,
hollow into which clouds are buried.

Listen to the hum as you barrel via concrete,
shrouded water bookended by light.

The asphalt has crumbled below
the wheels it meant to cushion,

no patch exists to stop the crack
beneath every revolution.

The flyover would be faster,
but you can't outrun the underpass;

you can't ascend the chasm, you can't
hold your breath and delve beneath.

The only way is through.
Through.

The Gift

The book arrives wrapped
in thin skin
hennaed with the tattoo

of an ancient text
stamped out
symbol by symbol—

painstaking work
I cannot decipher.
So much like you

to send the thrall
of beauty
I cannot decode,

veiled intent
I interpret
as *I miss you*

when what
you meant
was *good-bye.*

When You Ask about Karen

It's easier to diagnose her
as a mere side effect,
consequence of postpartum
that tethered me to interiors
for weeks—until her call,
thoughts of her enough to heat water,
wash away breast milk and spit-up,
the isolation I wore every day.

Easier to say we were nothing
more than sheets drenched
with infection we called love,
strain of lust I was ripe to contract,
easier than admit I signed up
for her auburn-tressed trial,
refused inoculation,
because I thought I knew the risks.

Easier to say she did not matter,
deny that some mornings
only her coffee-laced phone call
coaxed me out bed,
rather than tell you
I believed in us
with the innocence of a girl
I never was.

Easier to say
I never think of her,
that no splinter remains,

no shard or sliver,
no tiny cross-stitched
space within the expanse
of heart that now carries
your name.

What You Called to Say at Lunch

*Nine fossilized teeth found in Ethiopia are from a previously
unknown species of great ape.*

—*USA Today*, 2008

Your message spoke of a lost species
so old it had grown new again. Great apes
that ruled Ethiopia ten million years ago,
terrible teeth giving pause to science,
things we thought we knew about origins and limits.
I understood then why it took so long to find you,
why it took years to sort through variables,
identify the longing, harness it into tools
I needed to break it all down, fossils giving way
to answers, like the bones of that gorilla,
buried for eons, glorious, finally found.

Ink

I know the comfort
you take from your rituals—
now that our books
have intermingled
yours remain yours
favorite lines
underscored
in black ink
poured
from the same
pen, the same
twist and pop
of the cap
on the Cross
you refill
one fine point
at a time, stored
in the only purse
you've ever carried,

the bull prance
of your boots
on the scrape
that waits
for your soles
in the same spot
day after day,

the single brand
of eyeliner
you track down,

convinced
there is no other.

I keep
waiting
to become
indispensable—

the coat you mend,
pockets molded
by years
of your hands,

the scratch
on your vinyl,
the warp
on your cassettes,

flaws you overlook
for the sake
of love.

I want to be
the only one
who will do,

the one
you will never
replace.

Pulse: A Memorial in Driftwood, Cannon Beach, OR

We have crossed a continent
to cast forty-nine names into the sea
cuarenta y nueve nombres mangled
by anchormen—Flores, Paniagua, Sanfeliz—
on a beach strewn with the bones of giants:
Redwood, Sequoia, Sitka Spruce.
Behemoths that would not stay buried.

Before the ruined beauty of this necropolis
saplings cleaved to elders, grew
stronger in each other's arms
as they danced in darkened groves,
lit by the strobe of sunlight, dappled
limbs akimbo, unprepared for annihilation,
unprepared for the spilled sap, the glint
of the axe, the buzz saw, the prayers
planted at the root of their destruction.

I step over titans battered down
to driftwood, stripped of tannin and pulp,
bark bleached white as sheets and offer
forty-nine names to the sea
cuarenta y nueve nombres al mar.

Here I can believe the ocean
returns what she is given.

Solving the Crossword

For Elizabeth

We are new to one another, new to being us
yet old enough to know it always starts like this—

delicious to the point of delirium.
Still, we are more than that

and I'm surprised at all the ways
we fit, even when we don't,

each difference a study in alchemy, in balance,
in working through instead of out.

On our first flight together, I remember
those airplane rides before you, crosswords

I attempted alone, each puzzle unsolved,
abandoned to the next traveler.

Now, we work on solutions together—
mine our collective, break down

words to fill the emptiness within
rigid black boxes

with the precise mark
of your perfect, graphite script.

The poem "Entry" borrows its form from *The Oxford English Dictionary* and is informed by the content found at www. moscasdecolores.com.

The "wet foot, dry foot policy" is the informal name given to a 1996 agreement under which Cubans migrants to the United States who were intercepted at sea ("wet feet") were sent back to Cuba . . . while those who made it to U.S. soil ("dry feet") were allowed to remain in the United States. Undocumented Haitian migrants who reached U.S. shores were not automatically eligible for immigrant visas, or permanent residence, only Cubans. On January 12, 2017, President Barack Obama announced the immediate cessation of the wet foot, dry foot policy.

My participation in the *PINTURA : PALABRA* project, a multiyear initiative that provided me with access to the Smithsonian American Art Museum exhibit *Our America: The Latino Presence in American Art* as part of an ekphrastic writing workshop, provided the spark and inspiration for the poems "Unpacking the Suitcase," written after the installation *West Side Story Upside Down, Backwards, Sideways and Out of Focus (La Maleta de Futriaco Martinez)* by ADÁL, 2002, and "Topography," after *Siluetas Series* by Ana Mendieta, 1980.

The poem "Pulse: A Memorial in Driftwood, Cannon Beach, OR" was written in honor of the forty-nine people who died at the hands of a mass shooter on June 12, 2016, inside Pulse, a gay nightclub in Orlando, Florida.

ACKNOWLEDGMENTS

My deep-felt appreciation and eternal gratitude to the following people for their unwavering support of *Tortillera*—both the book and the poet:

Richard Blanco, Catherine Esposito Prescott, Jen Karetnick, and Nikki Moustaki, my ride-or-die poetry posse, whose keen advice, illuminating conversation, and enduring friendship have proved invaluable throughout the writing of this book;

Mi gente de *PINTURA : PALABRA*—Elisa Albo, Francisco Aragon, Silvia Curbelo, Roy Guzman, Mia Leonin, Rita M. Martinez, Alexandra Lytton Regalado, and Emma Trelles—for their fellowship and full-throttled support of *Tortillera* from its inception;

Deborah P. Briggs, Jonathan Plutzik, and the Betsy Hotel for providing me with a room of my own, sustenance and silence, during two Betsy Writer's Room residencies—the first in 2015, when I first started to assemble these poems into a manuscript, and the second in 2019, when the final poem fell into place;

The Elizabeth George Foundation for the gift of time through their generous funding in 2015;

Elizabeth and Sean-Michael, the two I love the best—the two who love me best, right back.

Many thanks to the following anthologies and literary journals in which some of these poems, at times in earlier incarnations, appeared:

The Antioch Review: "What the White Girl Asked at Our 20th High School Reunion"

The Best American Poetry Blog: "Entry"

Broad River Review: "Doing Without"

CALYX: A Journal of Art and Literature by Women: "Analfabeta"

The Collapsar: "At Least I Didn't Rape You"

The Comstock Review: "Ink"

Conte: A Journal of Narrative Writing: "Wet Foot, Dry Foot, 2002"

The Cossack Review: "Taking the Sunrise Tunnel" and "What They Don't Tell You at the Baby Shower"

Crab Orchard Review: "Inheritance"

The Damfino Journal: "The Really Good Dutch Oven"

Diverse Voices Quarterly: "Why Can't You Just Listen?" and "The Gift"

Fifth Wednesday Journal: "Coming Out to Mami"

Grabbed: Poets and Writers Respond to Sexual Assault, Empowerment and Healing (Beacon Press, 2020): "At Least I Didn't Rape You"

Hartskill Review: "I Did Not Take My Camera to Paris"

Home in Florida: Latinx Writers on the Politics of Belonging (University Press of Florida, in press): "Analfabeta," "Topography," and "Wet Foot, Dry Foot, 2002"

The Linden Avenue Literary Review: "Uncoupled," "Somnambulism 101: Never Wake a Talker," and "Pruning Black-Eyed Susans on the Day of Our Divorce"

Literary Mama: "Waiting to Be Discharged from the Maternity Ward"

Lunch Ticket: "When You Ask about Karen"

The Meadowland Review: "For Marlene, Who Asked Why I Switched Teams"

MiPoesias: American Cuban Issue: "Puta," "Quinceañera," and "What I Should Have Said, Instead"

Moon City Review: "Fourth Quarter"

Nebo: "I Don't Eat Plums Anymore" and "Memento Mori"

The Notre Dame Review: "Unpacking the Suitcase"

The Pedestal Magazine: "What You Called to Say at Lunch"

Pulse/Pulso: In Remembrance of Orlando (Damaged Goods Press, 2018): "Pulse: A Memorial in Driftwood, Cannon Beach, OR"

Rhino: "Entry"

The Seattle Review: "That Night at the Rack 'Em Room"

Slipstream Journal: "The Perfect Dress"

South Florida Poetry Journal: "Solving the Crossword," "Topography," and "What You Learn at the Track"

Spillway Journal: "Raisins in the Stuffing"

SWWIM: "Pulse: A Memorial in Driftwood, Cannon Beach, OR"

The Tishman Review: "Cuban-American Lexicon"

The Woven Tale Press: "Inheritance," "Coming Out to Mami," and "What You Called to Say at Lunch"